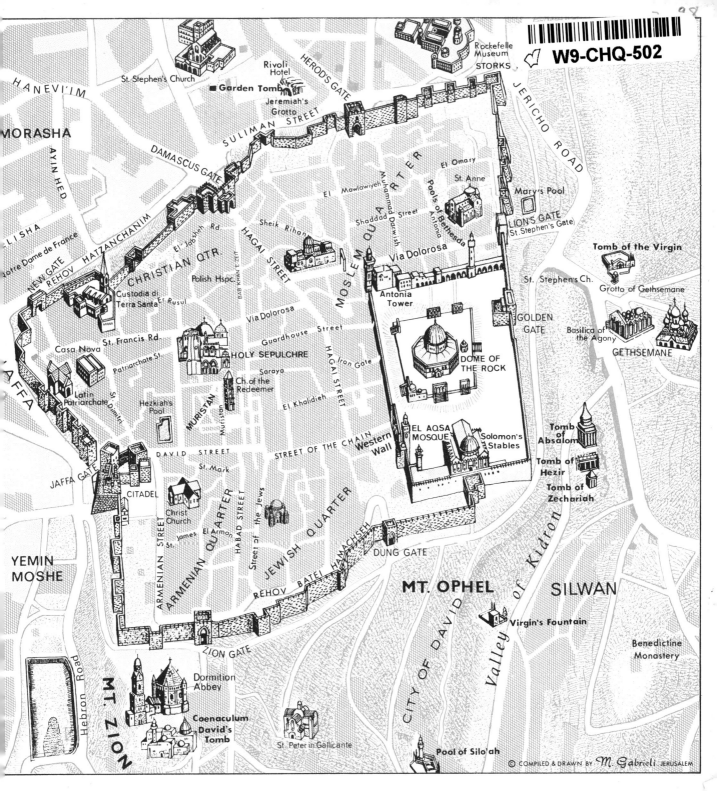

W9-CHQ-502

Pinnacle Books: Jerusalem

JERUSALEM

With 40 color plates by Werner Braun

Text by Gabriella Rosenthal

Distributed by

DOUBLEDAY & COMPANY, INC.
GARDEN CITY, NEW YORK

Translated by Zehava Albert and Eamonn Doyle

Library of Congress Catalog Card No. 68–27620
© 1968 by Wilhelm Andermann Verlag, Munich.
All rights reserved by publisher and author.
The printing blocks were produced by A. Gässler & Co., Munich.
The illustrations were printed by Stadlerdruck, Constance.
E. C. Baumann KG, Kulmbach, typeset and printed the text.
The art paper was provided by Scheufelen, Oberlenningen and
the book printing paper by Heinz Uhlemann, KG, Eltville.
The binding was done by Thomas-Buchbinderei, Augsburg.
Printed in Germany 168.

Jerusalem

No city is as familiar and none as mysterious as Jerusalem. Who does not carry in his heart a childhood image of "the city built on high"? Eighteen times besieged, conquered and destroyed, it always rose again revivified. But even when it lay utterly waste and the jackals prowled across its buried sanctuaries, people all over the world turned towards it in prayer and built a "heavenly" Jerusalem in their hearts.

Nor is there a logical reason why this particular city became great and survived. Many other cities lay nearer to the great trade routes, at more abundant springs and on more fertile soil. Some of these, bearing great and even older names — Jericho,

Sichem, which later became Nablus, Beit Sh'ean — exist to this day. But they have long ceased to exert their influence on the course of history. Jerusalem, high in the mountains of Judah on the very border between the arable land and the desert, is a city of pilgrimage for three great religions; a centre of science and research and again the capital of a sovereign state.

Is Jerusalem "Salem," a sacred city even when its king, Melchizedek, "who was a priest of the Most High God," brought out wine and bread to Abraham and blessed him as the chosen of the Lord? (Genesis 14, 18). To the ancients "holiness" had a different, a much more definite and almost more tangible meaning than the vague and varied sense in which we use it today. We are unable to fathom what was quite plain and manifest to them.

Let us then wander among the walls and streets of the city. And as we go, now overwhelmed by its diversity, now stirred by its loveliness, captivated by the endless colours of its life, puzzled by seeming paradoxes, we shall pause now and again to listen to the story of the stones under the golden light of Judea. We shall not solve their riddles, but perhaps we shall divine something of the holy mystery for which there are no words.

Zion, the City of David

David's decision to make Jerusalem his royal city was indeed a stratagem of genius. He had been king of Hebron for seven years, for five of them being king over all

Israel. Even so, in Hebron he was virtually a guest of the related Caleb clan, who held the region from the time of Joshua. Tribal concepts were still uppermost in the consciousness of the people. All the more did the recently formed kingdom stand in need of a national and royal centre, standing above clan allegiances.

A strip of Canaanite territory still lay between the northern Israelite territory and Samaria. It was controlled by the Jebusite city of Jerusalem, which covered the hill above the Gichon spring in the Kidron Valley, between the Mount of Olives and what is today called Mount Zion. A natural fortress, it was reinforced by well-built walls and strong defensive towers. A prolonged siege would have been necessary in order to overcome such a city; the Israelite army, however, was not experienced in this type of warfare. In a daring exploit, David's army commander, Joab, took the city from within (Chronicles 11, 4—8). According to Canaanite custom, its spring, lying just outside the walls, was walled and camouflaged. It could only be reached from within the city walls by means of a tunnel and staircase hewn into the rock. Joab and his soldiers succeeded in penetrating the outside fortification, entering the city through the rockshaft and conquering it without bloodshed or destruction, nor were the Canaanite inhabitants expelled. Indeed, for a long period the main body of civil service was drawn from them. For they were experts not only in building and administration but also in commerce. The Hebrew word "Kena'ani" — Canaanite — was long used as a synonym for "trader."

With the ceremonious removal of the Ark of the Covenant from Kiryiat Yearim — a distance of some ten miles — to David's City of Zion, this became the holy city of the promised land for all time (2 Samuel 6, 3).

The city of Zion, the Ophel, has vanished. Only some remains of the defensive walls and of a few buildings have been discovered. During the reign of Herod, stone was quarried from its site. The meaning of the names Jerusalem, Zion and Ophel, and their relationship to one another, are still not known. At a later period the name "Mount Zion" was given to the southwest hill above the Valley of Hinnom.

A Walk Around the Walls: Mount Zion

We start our walk at Jaffa Gate before the Citadel. The Valleys of Kidron and Hinnom form a natural moat around the city, connected only by a ridge in the northwest to the mountain plateau. This stretch of the city, being the weakest strategically, is therefore the most strongly fortified. The fortifications date, for the most part, from the time of the Mameluk rule during the 13th to the 16th centuries. Here, as in numerous places in the walls, the huge, rimmed Herodian ashlars stand out clearly from the later masonry. The great square Tower of Phasael was left intact when Titus razed the city in 70 A.D. to bear witness to posterity of what monstrous walls the emperor had conquered and destroyed. The upper storeys were added at a later period. The foundations lie deep beneath the moat. This is one of the three defensive towers — Phasael, Hyppicus and Mariamne — that protected the palace of Herod, which once stood on the site of the fortress. The Crusaders called it the Tower of David, and it became the personal fortress of the Royal Christian House of Jerusalem. At a later date the Turkish minaret within the fortress became known as the Tower of David.

1 The Citadel

2   *The Church of the Dormition on Mount Zion*   3   *The Hall of the Last Supper (Coenaculum)*

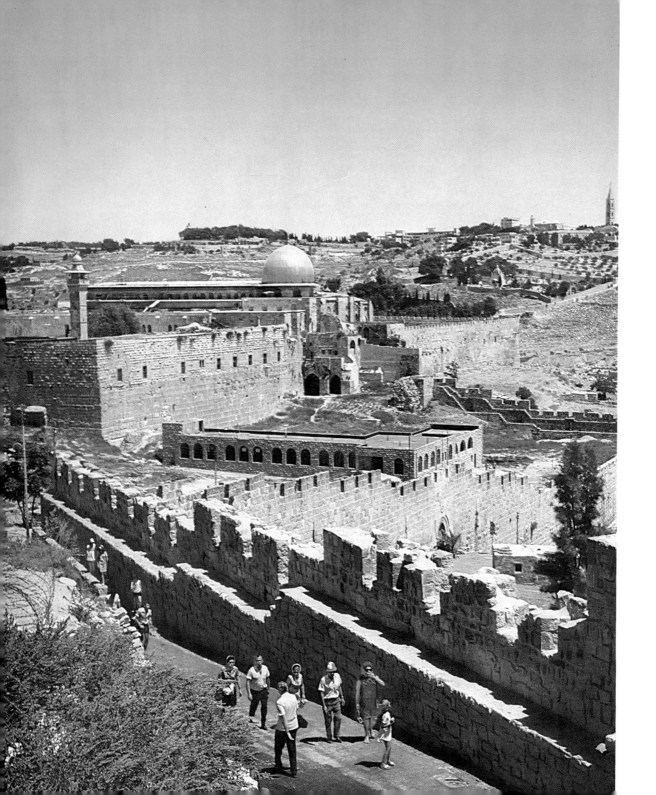

4 *The Southeast Section of the Wall*   5 *View of the Southeast Corner of the Wall from the Valley of Kidron*

6
*On the
Mount of Olives*

7

he Garden of Gethsemane

Between the Jaffa Gate and the Citadel lies an open space. Sultan Abdul Hamid had the walls breached when his powerful ally, the German Kaiser, visited the country and the city in the autumn of 1898. The impressive show of the Imperial cortège must not be allowed to get jammed in the narrow gateway.

The walls and gates received their present form when Sultan Suleiman the Magnificent restored and rebuilt them towards the middle of the 16th century. From the period of the later kingdom until the destruction of the city by Titus, all of Mount Zion as far as Ophel lay within the city walls. Its most recent wall cuts across the top of Mount Zion and its southern slope, then joins up with the old foundations.

The tradition that places the Last Supper and the miracle of Pentecost on the heights of Mount Zion can be traced back to the 4th century. In the 7th century the site of Mary's house began to be venerated here; a medieval Jewish legend holds that this spot is also the site of David's Tomb.

In the year 390, the great "Hagia Zion," the "Mother of all Churches," was erected here. Thirty pairs of pillars divided the enormous interior of the basilica into five aisles. Encompassing the site of the Last Supper and the Pentecost Chapel, the building stretched from a point near the city walls, a few yards behind the present rotunda of the Church of the Dormition, up to and including the complex of King David's Tomb.

Here again the tragic pattern of the country's history repeats itself: destruction by the Persians in 614, reconstruction, destruction by the mad Caliph Hakim in the 11th century, reconstruction by the Crusaders and, finally, destruction by the Saracens.

In 1335, forty-four years after the collapse of the Christian Kingdom, the royal house of Aragon succeeded in obtaining rights of worship for the Franciscans at some of the Holy Places, and permission to build a small monastery for the order on Mount Zion. A few years later the friars were able to erect the noble Chamber of the Last Supper over King David's Tomb, the only high-Gothic building in the country, probably a work of Cypriot craftsmen.

The Turks, who succeeded the Mameluks as rulers of the country at the beginning of the 16th century, expelled the friars and transformed King David's Tomb and the Chamber of the Last Supper into two small mosques; the Moslems venerate King David as the prophet "Nebi Da'oud." An over-ornate prayer niche now blocks the central window. Until 1948 entry was only rarely permitted to Christians or Jews. Then the southwestern hill became Israeli territory. The holy place, however, retained its status as a mosque, and the Moslem religious authorities still allow only silent worship.

As in former times when access to the Temple Wall was denied to the Jews, and until the reunification of Jerusalem, King David's Tomb became the main Jewish place of pilgrimage, for at least it lay within the confines of the biblical city.

Two of the walls at this site were erected on foundations and parts of a wall of a synagogue dating from the Roman era. It is assumed that one of the first Judeo-Christian communities assembled here for prayer during that time, and perhaps in the presence of the apostles.

Only the complex of "Nebi Da'oud" existed here when the Sultan made the gift of the adjoining land to the German Kaiser. It was then placed under the authority of the

18

archiepiscopal See of Cologne. In the spring of 1910, the Benedictine church and abbey "Dormitio Mariae" was consecrated. The pedestal of one of the side altars in the crypt of this church is a massive white marble stump — the last fragment of one of the sixty magnificent pillars of the Hagia Zion.

Shortly after the founding of the State of Israel, when Mount Zion was still considered the holiest ground in Israel, the Martef Hasho'a — "The Cave of the Holocaust," a deeply moving memorial to the victims of Nazi Germany — was built near King David's Tomb.

Our way now leads through pine groves down into the valley, past the "House of Caiphas," in full view of the Mount of Olives. Above the city wall rises the golden cupola of the Dome of the Rock, and the small, silvery dome of the Aksa Mosque.

The road runs above the new houses of the village of Silwan, which stand on the Acropolis of the Jebusite city. The cleft of the valley between the city of David and Temple Mount was filled in by command of King Solomon, the work being carried out by the men of Ephraim. The king himself appointed the young and gifted Jeroboam Ben Nabat as technical adviser. But Jeroboam put himself at the head of a revolt of his countrymen against the harsh labour laws that removed able-bodied men from their homes for months at a time. The revolt was suppressed, the work continued, and Jeroboam fled to Egypt. During the reign of Rehoboam, the weak heir of Solomon, Jeroboam returned as the first king of the secessionist kingdom of Israel (1 Kings 11, 26—40 and 12, 20).

The honey-coloured wall runs ruler-straight along the height of the Temple Mount, broken only by the Byzantine Golden Gate. There is a legend that the Messiah will enter the city here and lay claim to the Temple Area. For that reason the Moslems prudently walled up this gateway.

The Mount of Olives and the Rock Tombs

The summit of the Mount of Olives is covered with houses, churches, monasteries and a modern hotel. The slope below is covered with thousands of Jewish graves, each marked with a stone plinth. At the end of the bridge over the valley stands the Italian Church of the Agony built in Byzantine style. Farther up, making an oasis of shade, are the millennial olive trees of a grove which in the time of Jesus was called Gat Shamen — the oil presses — the Garden of Gethsemane. From among the trees arises the little Russian church of Mary Magdalene with its seven onion-topped towers, a charming picture-book whimsy. Deep in the valley lies the Church of the Tomb of Mary with its fine Crusader façade.

On the southern slope, massive stone monuments have been chiselled out of the rock face and mausoleums hewn into the mountainside. People called them the tombs of Absalom, of Zachariah and of the prophetess Hulda. In actual fact they are the tombs of prominent Jerusalem families, monuments in the classical style, which, however, would be unthinkable in southern Europe. They recall the architectural fantasies of Petra. Heavier, and more sparsely ornamented, they were indeed built during the same era — that of the Hasmoneans — which commenced in 165 B.C. with the capture of Jerusalem by Judas Maccabeus and his brother, and concluded with the seizure of power by Herod, about 120 years later. The war of the Maccabees also marked the intensification of the long struggle between Judah and Greece. Alexander's Panhellenic dream had long become true in Egypt and in the coastal cities, where Greek mercantile colonies had existed since ancient times. The local gods were worshipped in their Hellenized form, and Greek was both the lingua franca and the language of the literate world. The native culture continued to exist, mainly in its rural form.

The Jews would not have resisted the dominant classical culture — many, in fact, had already adopted it — had it not threatened the sphere of God. Then, as before and later, they were quite prepared to make peace with the foreign administrative power as long as their religious freedom was respected. However, the Seleucid king, Antiochus Epiphanes IV, a fanatical Hellenist, went so far as to forbid the sanctification of the Sabbath, circumcision, and even the teaching of the Law. Rebellion broke out in the small town of Modi'in, in the northern foothills of Judah, and flared into war. After three years of fierce fighting, Jerusalem was conquered, the Temple purified and the cult restored.

A strict, unworldly theocracy, however, would not have suited the newly united, vigorous nation with its conflicting trends and the political awareness with which it strove to gain its place among the nations of the Middle East. Inevitably the cities were built in a style that had been used for generations from Africa to the Black Sea. Books and chronicles could not be written in a language other than that of the readers. What matters is not that the Books of the Maccabees were written in Greek, but that they perpetuate the Jewish spirit adapted to a new mode of life, yet retaining the essence of the Covenant with Jehovah.

Let us now return to our wanderings. The Valley of Kidron forms part of the gigantic necropolis that, during Jesus' lifetime, was far larger than the city of the living, which it enclosed in a wide arc. According to Jewish law, cemeteries are not allowed to be laid out inside the city walls. Arable land being scarce and precious, the tombs were hewn into the relatively soft limestone rock. Fine burial chambers and niches can be found miles away from the old city — sometimes with the great rolling stone still in place, as the one mentioned in the description of Christ's resurrection.

The Mount of Olives and Mount Scopus are actually a single range, and from the northern heights the view extends from the Dead Sea into Samaria. On the long, sprawling summit stands the Auguste Victoria Hospital, erected by the German Emperor as a Protestant pilgrims' hospice and named after the Empress. Imperial caprice decreed that it should be built as a Central German fortress, and thus it stands, with its pointed gables and squat towers, incongruous and alien beneath this sky. Adjoining it are the buildings of the first Hebrew University and of the first Hadassah Hospital. (The latter were designed by Erich Mendelsohn.) On the northernmost height there is a military cemetery in which are interred British, Australian and New Zealand soldiers who died in Palestine during the First World War.

A Walk Around the Walls:
From the Lions' Gate to the Jaffa Gate

Let us turn again to our left, towards the city wall. The road climbs up to the Lions' Gate, named after the heraldic felines on its façade. Like several of the gates, it also has a second name: St. Stephen's Gate. Tradition has it that Christianity's first martyr was led through it on his way to execution. The bullet and shell scars are of recent origin: for the first time in its long and war-harassed history, Jerusalem was assaulted and taken from the Kidron Valley on June 7th, 1967.

We climb the ascending road to the corner tower of Burj Laklak — the "Storks' Tower" — and then turn westward. On the hill opposite stands the Rockefeller Museum, which contains a wealth of archaeological treasures — dating from the Stone Age through the biblical era to the time of the Crusades. Dozens of shells have scarred the smooth, white masonry of the fine building. Since its inauguration in 1939 it has stood twice in the firing line: in 1948 and in 1967.

The city wall now runs over masses of piled-up rocks, and the new city is separated from it only by the width of a two-lane highway. Where once stood the elegant Roman residential quarter of Bethesda, there is now a noisy bus terminal, littered with rubbish and adjoining a gloomy, craggy hill pitted with deep caves — the site of the "Garden Tomb" which some believe to be Golgotha; we pass along prosaic, bustling streets and a dusty parking lot used both for motor vehicles and beasts of burden. But is this not the way cities survive?

The charming little Flower Gate, also called Herod's Gate, set with graceful stone medallions, stands at a fateful spot — the strategically weakest point of the city. It was from here that Nebuchadnezzar took the city, and here the Roman soldiers forced their way into the town. At this spot Godfrey of Bouillon succeeded in manoeuvring his "château de bois" up to the wall — the tall wooden rolling tower that was covered with the hides of freshly slaughtered animals to protect it from "Greek fire," the secret incendiary weapon of the Saracens: across a light footbridge thrown from above, the first Franks stormed into the city.

Soon Damascus Gate, the most ornate of the city gates, is reached. Beneath it was found the Herodian gate. Now the road climbs upwards towards the great complex of Notre Dame de France. Here again, the scars of the drawn-out fighting in 1948 are clearly evident. The New Gate opposite is little more than a breach in the wall. Its Arabic name — Abdul Hamid Gate — points to its recent origin. A short distance and we have reached Jaffa Road. The wall curves southwards and we return to our starting point.

The Temple Area

From the eastern hills, the view of the city spread out below is one of startling beauty. Inside the walls, high above the Kidron Valley, lies the Temple Area. At its centre, like a great, preciously cut, gold-set turquoise, rises the Dome of the Rock. Pine-trees and cypresses encircle fountains; well-houses and pavilions are dispersed in

9   *The Temple Mount at Sunrise*

11
The Lions' Gate

13 *The Dome of the Rock*

14 *The Solemn Friday Service in the Aksa Mosque*

15 *The Damascus Gate*

enchanting asymmetry. The great Aksa Mosque borders on the central part of the southern enclosure. Four minarets rise above the area. The two sides facing the city are lined with graceful mansions and palaces. Temple Mount rose again as "the Furthest Sanctuary" of Islam in the beauty and majesty befitting the site of unfathomable mystery.

Here, on a summer's day almost three thousand years ago, the Jebusite Arauna rode his threshing cart around the golden heaps of barley — as the farmers in the mountain villages still do today — and saw with astonishment the aged king and his retinue ascend from the city of Ophel. David had come to purchase the land, and the price agreed on was 50 ounces of silver, the cattle to be included with the land. The glory of building the Temple was not granted to David, but he erected a great sacrificial altar here (2 Samuel 24, 18).

In 967 B.C., in the fourth year of his reign, King Solomon began building the Temple. The Bible tells us in great detail about the preparatory work and the materials: the beautifully hewn stones which came from a quarry that can still be reached through a gateway between the Damascus Gate and Herod's Gate; of the enormous amount of ore, gold and cedar-wood, and of the organization of the work of construction (1 Kings, chapters 5 and 6). At that time the predominantly rural nation had neither architects nor craftsmen capable of undertaking a project of such magnitude and splendour. It was their Phoenician allies who not only delivered the cedar trees tied onto huge rafts, but also provided the architects, technicians and craftsmen. The Phoenician-Canaanite style elements can easily be recognized in the detailed descriptions of the basic construction and the ornamentation, as in the tripartition of the shrine and the decoration of the Tabernacle with the golden cherubim. The construction of the temple complex lasted thirteen years and encompassed courtyards, around which stood the living quarters of the priests and Levites on duty, the congregational halls, the treasury and the storehouses; the altars, one of which — called the "brazen sea" — was shaped like an enormous basin, "whose rim resembled the bloom of a lily" and which rested on twelve steers cast in bronze; and the sanctuary itself, with its three halls, the last of which, the Holy of Holies, housed the Ark of the Covenant.

Under the hapless Rehoboam, Solomon's heir, the kingdom split. Despite all the efforts of David and Solomon, people still clung to ancient tribal loyalties — which were skilfully fostered and exploited by the enemies of the royal house. Under the rule of Jeroboam, who returned from exile after Solomon's death, the northern tribes now formed their own kingdom — Israel. This included the fertile plains of Sarona and Jesre'el, part of the coastal plain and the rich Jordan Valley, and the mountains and plains of Samaria and Galilee. Apart from the only partially fertile mountain land of Judah — whose loyalty to the royal house remained unquestionably firm — the southern kingdom now encompassed only the tiny hill territory of the tribe of Benjamin, and in the south the lands of the small, still semi-nomadic tribe of Simeon on the edge of the desert.

From the hills, which only yesterday encircled the glittering capital of a great power, it was now possible to distinguish the borders of the Kingdom of Judah in three directions. Much of the golden trappings of the Temple and of the treasure was sent to the ruling Pharaoh as a tribute to save the city from destruction (1 Kings 14, 25). Jerusalem became a city of priests. This does not mean that at all times its interests were thus best served. The prophets themselves inveighed often and sharply against the priestly caste. Nor did the political situation remain static: kings of the house of David still arose who expanded the frontiers of their kingdom, and Judah did not vanish entirely from the international political scene. But the driving force and the place among the powers of the Middle East was assumed by the northern kingdom. It was the kings of Israel who continued the policy of alliance with the Phoenicians, who led their chariot regiments against Syria, and whose friendship was sought after. However, neither from Samaria nor from Jesre'el, but "from Zion emanated the Law, and the word of God from Jerusalem" (Isaiah 2, 3). Here the tradition was maintained, the chronicles written, and the laws not only preserved but continually re-adapted to the changing and developing circumstances.

The kings of the house of David ruled until the destruction of the kingdom, the city and the Temple in August, 586 B. C., described so vividly by Jeremiah, who was an eye-witness (Kings 25, Jeremiah, Lamentations). Forty years later, the Persian King Cyrus, who had conquered Babylon, allowed the Jews to return. Only the bravest, the idealists — and certainly not the richest, although these generously supported the project — dared to embark on this undertaking. Tradition had been preserved, but many had found a new home in exile and acquired both respect and high position. To rebuild a ruined city and resettle a wasteland is an arduous task. It was made even harder by the Samaritan inhabitants, and time and again hampered by political intrigue. When the main altar had been rebuilt, the construction of a new temple commenced. "Many of the priests and Levites and heads of families, who had known the earlier temple, wept aloud as the ground was broken for this one;

many others, however, broke into loud cries of jubilation. It was not possible to distinguish the shouts of joy from the open weeping of the people" (Ezra 12—23).

In the year 515 B. C., the new Temple was consecrated. King Darius had not only contributed to its construction, he also sent back to Jerusalem those vessels of the Temple cult which had been carried away by Nebuchadnezzar and could still be found. Later the walls were rebuilt under the most arduous conditions. Half of the men had to be constantly on the alert and armed to repel attacks, and even the stone-carriers bore arms.

Nothing is known of the shape and aspect of either city or Temple, which can only have been very modest compared to those of former times. The chronicled history of the Old Testament ends with the Book of Nehemiah around the middle of the fifth century B. C. Then follow centuries of obscurity, and only vague indications from rare sources shed a dim, uncertain light at long intervals. Alexander the Great appears to have appointed a governor and endowed the High Priest with the rank of ethnarch, or people's representative, and the city suffered during the Seleucid wars. Only with the Books of the Maccabees and the years just before the reconquest of Jerusalem in the winter of the year 165 B. C. does a continuous historical chronology begin again. But it is still not possible to visualize the Temple Area as it must have looked 350 years after its consecration and during the Hasmonean era. A clear image of the city only re-emerges during the reign of Herod the Great. It is so closely associated with the person of this evil and despotic monarch that a brief sketch of him would seem to be appropriate.

Around the beginning of the first century B.C. the Hasmonean King Alexander

Jannai had forced the Edomites to accept Judaism. Herod was born a Jew into a prominent Edomite family about 73 B. C. His father Antipas was a high court official and the *de facto* ruler at the court of the weak King Hyrcanos. Already in his youth, the son had proved himself to be a gifted, unscrupulous and arrogant "strategos" of Galilee. A politician of genius, he succeeded in becoming "rex socius et amicus." As long as he remained in favour with Rome he was thus free to rule at will in his own kingdom. His passion for building, the maintenance of his extravagant court, the expensive gifts he lavished on the neighbouring Roman governors and his contact men in Rome itself, required tremendous financial resources, which were extracted from the people by the laying-on of ever new and increasingly burdensome taxes. When these could no longer be extorted, other means were employed. After the bloody conquest of Jerusalem with an army of mercenaries in 37 B.C., he had forty of the richest men executed and their fortunes confiscated. Strange as it may seem, this shrewd man-of-the-world, who affected every fashion decreed in Rome, who built Caesarea as a cultural centre on classical lines, never denied his Jewishness: he even flaunted it ostentatiously on occasion. Following the conquest of Jerusalem, with its horrifying aftermath, he devoted himself to rebuilding the city on a grandiose scale. The city arose in the oriental-Hellenistic style, that wove its wealth of imaginative invention and baroque playfulness freely around the pure classical concepts.

Never before had such walls and towers been seen in the country. As Jerusalem assumed its new aspect, it was inevitable that the whole of the Temple complex be rebuilt in a manner commensurate with the new surroundings — larger and more sumptuous than the Temple of Solomon, which still lived in the memory of the people.

As the Temple neared completion, Herod, true to his sinister genius, commanded that an enormous golden Roman eagle be mounted on the façade. Those young rebels who tore down the heathen symbol were brutally executed. As a further insult, the city's fortress Antonia was erected to tower over the Temple Area, and from its upper windows the garrison troops could view the courtyards of the Temple, to which access was denied to non-Jews. Thus a splendid sanctuary arose, mocking the spirit to which it was consecrated. Fires burnt upon the altars, the people thronged the magnificent colonnaded courtyards: day after day the solemn ritual was celebrated in conformity with the age-old laws — even if the High Priest was a puppet appointed by the king.

The true spirit that was to survive, however, was fostered only in the great "hall of hewn stones" where the plenary sessions of the Sanhedrin were held. This body had long ceased to exert any secular authority; it was kept alive in the classrooms of the teachers of Scriptures and in the synagogues, where prayers were offered at the hours of the ritual sacrifices. There was even a synagogue in the Temple Area itself. Not everyone could or would attend the spectacular archaic rites which actually had a purpose. How often in those hours of quiet devotion must the prayers for the dead have been recited for those murdered by the king, among them his wife, the beautiful Hasmonean Princess Mariamne, and her two sons.

After Herod's death in the year 4 B. C., the reins of government passed into the hands of the Roman procurators, who preferred to take up residence in gay Caesarea Maritima, where the theatre programmes were far more varied, the hippodromes, baths and gymnasia more luxurious, and life more pleasant and less complicated. The predominantly Syrian-Greek population ("Greek" meaning a complete assimilation to Hellenism) caused the authorities no trouble. Only three times a year, during Passover, Shavuoth, and the Feast of the Tabernacles, did the governors visit the capital, accompanied by a large military force. While tens of thousands of pilgrims were thronging the city, the ever tense and uneasy political situation was likely to become dangerous. The magnificent city built by Herod stood only for one hundred years.

Christ's admonition to "give to Caesar what is Caesar's" accorded with the moderate attitude of responsible and politically minded people. There may at first, perhaps, have been a lack of understanding, but in the final analysis it was the sheer malevolence and ruthlessness of the Roman administration that drove the people into fierce opposition and, in A. D. 66, unleashed the appalling four-year war of annihilation that reached its bloody conclusion with the dreadful siege and capture of the starving capital. It was in vain that Titus ordered the Temple to be spared. The enraged legionaries were uncontrollable. For minutes the majestic building appeared to glow from within before it collapsed. "Streams of blood," reported the eye-witness and historian Josephus Flavius, "quenched the leaping flames." It was the ninth day in the month of Av, by the Jewish calendar the same midsummer day on which the Temple of Solomon had been destroyed 656 years earlier.

Sixty years after the razing of Jerusalem, the people who had remained in the province of Judah still dreamt of the holy city's resurrection. Throughout the Diaspora they prayed for it — in Kyrene and Alexandria, in Mesopotamia, Persia, Greece, in Rome and on the Rhine. Pilgrims were continually stealing into the Roman military camp that stood on the former site of the city, bribing the soldiers for permission to pray at the ruined western wall of the Temple and at the sites of Christ's miracles. Though no fanatic, the Emperor Hadrian was an uncompromising Panhellenist. He regarded anything that did not, or would not, fit into the classical conception of culture and philosophy as barbarism. While the borders of the Empire appeared forever secure, such dissenting groups were apt to undermine it from within. These stubborn monotheists who were now scattered throughout the world, who prayed for the resurrection of a rebellious city that had been destroyed long ago, and continually returned to the site where the tenth legion was camped must be crushed. Thus, the Emperor had salt ploughed into the Temple Area and ordered a new city to be built on the site — no longer "Yerushalayim," whose name would now be obliterated forever — but Aelia Capitolina. The Jews and also the Christians who still lived in the surrounding districts saw the scaffolding rise on Temple Mount. Rumours began to circulate: Jerusalem is being rebuilt! And then they saw the Temple of Jupiter arising from the Temple Area.

Laws which recalled those of Epiphanes had embittered the population. The heathen temple on the site of the Holy of Holies, of God's manifestation, was too much to bear. In A. D. 133 rebellion broke out under the leadership of Simon Bar Kochba. For three years guerilla warfare raged before it could be put down with the aid of troops withdrawn from Britain. Rome's vengeance was as merciless as the war had been. In the following centuries Jewish life ceased to exist in the surroundings of Jerusalem. The dream of a Jewish State only began to take shape once more towards the end

17 View of the Old City towards the East

18 The "Prison of Christ"   19 The Via Dolorosa with the "Ecce Homo Arch"

Candle St.
outside
Courtya
of the Chur
of
Holy Sepulch

22

The Crusader Façade
the Church of the Ho
Sepulchre

23
The Chapel
of St. Helena

of the last century. The only remaining evidence of Aelia Capitolina, whose name has long been forgotten together with its gods, are the stones with which the Western Wall has been repaired, thus preserving it as the sanctuary of the scattered people; parts of a triumphal gateway which the people of Jerusalem who no longer remembered the Roman Emperor called the "Ecce Homo Arch;" and the marvellous pillars of the Temple of Jupiter which support the roof and cupola of the Dome of the Rock.

It is not known just how long the Temple of Jupiter existed; perhaps it was changed into a church. However, it had apparently disappeared when, in the sixth century, the Emperor Justinian commanded that a church in honour of Mary and a hospice be erected on the south side of the Temple. These were later destroyed by the Persians. In 629 the Emperor Heraclius succeeded in regaining control of the east, but this was to endure only for a short while. By the end of the same year, the Patriarch Sophronius complained that it was no longer possible to hold the usual Christmas celebrations in nearby Bethlehem, since mounted hordes from Arabia were making the area unsafe. They were the first campaigning vanguard of the Moslems. Five years later the great conquest began, and early in the year 638 Sophronius received the Caliph Omar in Jerusalem with full ceremony.

"Glory to Him who carried his servant by night from the Sacred Place of Worship to the Far Distant Place of Worship whose surroundings We have blessed . . ." Thus begins the seventeenth Surah of the Koran, the "Night's Journey," during which the Prophet rose up to stand before the face of God from the "Far Distant Place of

24 *The Golgotha Altar in the Church of the Holy Sepulchre*

Worship," el Masjid el Aqsa — meaning distant from Mecca — and returned in the same night. This site is the Temple Area in Jerusalem.

The inhabitants of the city looked on with astonishment as the Commander of the Faithful and his warlike followers cleared away the rubble and refuse from the square with their own hands. Strange conquerors! They venerated Moses, the Patriarchs, Solomon, David and Jesus as prophets. They included Jews and Christians in the "Family of the Book," allowing them to continue the practice of their religion. They were only required to pay a poll tax which, however, was levied only on men. Whoever wished to leave the city and the country could do so, taking his belongings with him, under the protection of an escort.

About sixty years later, under the Ommyad Caliph Abd el-Malik, the Temple Area arose again with a splendour that made men's hearts beat somewhat faster. The summit rock, the site of the "Night's Journey," was enclosed by the Dome of the Rock. The church of Justinian was rebuilt as a mosque — two aisles on either side obliterated the cruciform shape of the ground-plan.

The warriors of Islam from Hejaz had looked upon the classical and late-Roman ruins in wonderment. The spirit of classical forms remained alien to them. With the same fiery energy with which they had created a new form of monotheism suited to themselves — and soon to millions of others — while recognizing and incorporating the principles of the "Family of the Book," they availed themselves of the obsolete Hellenistic and old Persian architectural elements to re-create them within a new concept and style. The Dome of the Rock was the first great building of Islam — and perhaps the greatest to this day.

(The term "Mosque of Omar" makes no more sense than, for example, the "Tower of David." The building has no connection with Omar, nor is it a mosque. The Koranic name of the Temple Area was later applied to the Aksa Mosque alone, and the Area became known as "Haram e-Sherif" — the Exalted Enclave.)

During the thirteen hundred years of its existence, the building inevitably underwent alterations and repairs. The basic form, however, remained unchanged. For centuries it inspired architects the world over. Charlemagne took it as a model for his royal chapel at Aix-la-Chapelle. During the time of the Christian Kingdom of Jerusalem, when travel and pilgrimage to and from the Holy Land became livelier than ever, octagonal churches were being built in Italy, Germany, France and England. Frederick II was particularly fascinated by this architectural form. The Order of the Teutonic Knights, which was closely allied to the Imperial House, carried it far into Prussia. The Dome of the Rock appears in Raphael's "Sposalizio" and in Hubert van Eyck's "The Three Marys at the Tomb of Jesus".

It was still completely faced with marble. The glittering ceramic ornamentation was a contribution of Suleiman the Magnificent. In 1955 the unbelievably elaborate and artistic tile facing was restored — again a gift of Turkey.

At the Aksa Mosque, by contrast, a long history of renovations, alterations and earthquakes is clearly evident. The magnificent entrance hall, with its seven arches, was built in 1236 by a successor of Salah Eddin. The central aisles still recall the plan of the ancient Church of Mary. The complex and lofty building can accommodate five thousand worshippers. After the sanctuaries in Mecca and Medina, the Haram e-Sherif is the holiest in Islam. Princes used to sweep the great halls, wash the walls and pillars with rosewater, and stand at the doors distributing alms. Each of the lovely small buildings that have arisen in the Temple Area in the course of the centuries has its own legend.

The graceful palaces that house the administration, the archives, libraries, teaching centres and civil courts, and a row of residential buildings that borders the Area on the city side, were built between the 13th and 16th centuries, the era of the Mameluk reign. The most splendid of the entrance gates and many beautiful private and public buildings in the adjoining quarters were also erected during this period, one of continuous feuding and revolts of the soldier kings who, surprisingly, were at the same time the most generous patrons of the arts and sciences.

In July 1099 blood poured over the steps of the Haram e-Sherif and lay in pools in the halls and water basins. The accumulated tensions caused by the waging of the Crusade and the hardships of the siege during the merciless summer heat erupted in an orgy of slaughter. In vain Tancred and Bohemond handed over their pennants as a pledge to the inhabitants who had sought refuge in the sanctuaries. The blood-crazed soldiers massacred thousands who had sought the protection of the shrines. At nightfall on their way to the Te Deum in the Church of the Holy Sepulchre, the victors stepped over heaps of corpses. The goal had been reached, the tomb of Christ was conquered. (It should be mentioned that Christians had freely conducted their religious services in the Holy Sepulchre until the imminent approach of the Crusader army caused their expulsion from the city.) What saved the victors themselves from pestilence and disease was the Roman sewer system, which still functioned perfectly.

During the 88-year period in which Jerusalem was the capital of the Christian

Kingdom, a golden cross crowned the Dome of the Rock. It seems that the Crusaders regarded this building as having been the Temple of Solomon, since they named it the "Templum Domini." In the year 1118, a newly formed order of knights was permitted to install its mother house in the Aksa Mosque; the members of the order thereafter called themselves the "Knights Templars." Their task was to provide a military escort for the pilgrims. Like the Knights Hospitallers and the Teutonic Order at a later period, they comprised a powerful contingent of the Christian army. Their fatal separatist policy contributed in no small measure to the downfall of the city and the kingdom.

In July 1187, the Christian army was disastrously defeated at the "Horns of Hittin," not far from the Sea of Galilee, and on the 2nd of October, the anniversary of the Prophet's "Night's Journey," Salah Eddin entered Jerusalem. The crescent was once again affixed to the Dome of the Rock. A week later the Friday service was again conducted in the Aksa Mosque.

During the negotiations, Salah Eddin did full justice to his fame as a humane and magnanimous ruler. While the plans for withdrawal and the amount of ransom were being worked out, the rights and property of the vanquished were carefully guarded. Those not able to raise enough money were nevertheless released on payment of an extremely small sum. (A few years later, Richard the Lion-Hearted executed hundreds of Moslem hostages when the ransom from Salah Eddin was delayed.)

The Orthodox and Syrian Christians, the Copts and the Armenians remained in the city. They even welcomed the new regime. They much preferred the poll tax that was now demanded of them to the rule of the Franks, who had alienated their sympathies by their overbearing demeanour and their treatment of orientals as second-class citizens.

All Christian constructions and alterations to the Haram e-Sherif were now removed, with the exception of the great baronial hall which the Knights Templars had built onto the Aksa Mosque and which has since served as a women's mosque. At the same time the Sultan had the shrines restored to their former shape. The interior of the cupola of the Dome of the Rock was decorated with magnificent stuccowork and the marble facings were renewed.

The Via Dolorosa and the Church of the Holy Sepulchre

Directly behind the Lions' Gate lies St. Anne's Monastery of the White Fathers. It is the site of the pool of Bethesda, where Jesus healed the paralytic (John 5, 2—10). A later tradition places the house of Mary's birth here. The interior of the magnificent Crusaders' Church is temporarily covered with scaffolding and is being repaired. During the recent war, fighting took place near the Lions' Gate. Close to it is the Franciscan Monastery of the Flagellation, with the order's famed Bible Institute. The Chapel of the Scourging is the first station of the Via Dolorosa. Exactly how far the Via Dolorosa coincides with the Path to Calvary is a disputed question. The assumption that the Praetorium from which Jesus was led was a part of the fortified complex of the Antonia seems to have substance and is widely shared in circles connected with research. The immense square building, with its four solid corner towers, doubtlessly bordered on the southern side of the present-day Via Dolorosa. After the Franciscan monastery we reach the Greek convent of the "Prison of Christ." Here one descends into underground corridors and chambers hewn out of the rock — the largest of these served an earlier Christian community as a place of worship. As with many other buildings on the narrow lanes, arches and flying buttresses support the walls. A closer scrutiny of the "Ecce Homo Arch" at the Monastery of the Sisters of Zion reveals that the small building supported by it rests on a finely vaulted and chiselled arch. Below the building, tracks of Roman roads have been uncovered, running north from the Antonia. The paving stones are grooved to prevent horses from slipping. Enormous water cisterns from the Herodian period are still in use. In the church of the Sisters of Zion, which is somewhat above the level of the ancient streets, the Ecce Homo Arch continues, and it becomes clear that this is the centre piece of a triumphal arch erected to celebrate the "final victory" of Hadrian over Elohim, Jesus, and Jerusalem.

Between monastery buildings, antique and souvenir shops and through shady archways, the Via Dolorosa climbs to the bustling bazaar at the "Street of the Christians," which leads to a covered, descending passage. In front of narrow, huddled-together shops hang bundles of rosaries made of olive wood and mother-of-pearl, strings of coloured glass beads from Hebron and wreaths of tapers — white, coloured and decorated with gold — and the peculiar, spade-shaped candles adorned with golden scrolls. Incense grains are displayed in little bowls, carefully assorted according to quality.

We reach the court of the Church of the Holy Sepulchre. Dismayed, even shocked, the visitor pauses — is this the goal of countless pilgrims? The first impression is painfully contrary to the vision he has been harbouring of the site of awesome mystery. The façade is hidden by supports and scaffolding, building stones lie piled in the yard, labourers push wheelbarrows through the crowds of tourists and pilgrims, bawling to make themselves heard above the hammering of the stonemasons. Nor does the din abate inside the Church. In the rotunda and in the sanctuaries, differing styles bewilder the mind — ranging as they do from the Byzantine and the medieval to late rococo and the heavy pseudo-renaissance of the European nineteenth century. Stairs lead up and down, here in shadow and there beneath a cluster of golden lamps. Tourists and worshippers wander amidst a pandemonium of hammering and sawing. Has the pilgrim arrived at an inopportune hour? Recalling the history of the Church of the Holy Sepulchre, one realizes that visitors rarely found it tranquil and intact. Tremendous concentration has almost always been necessary if one wished to find here what one sought. We should pause here for a moment and might briefly recapitulate the history of the site, so that order may take over from chaos, the wealth of ornamentation fall into perspective, and the essential spirit emerge from the confusion.

The identification of the site of Golgotha goes back to the Empress Helena, who had the complex of tombs, chambers and cisterns excavated from beneath an altar of Venus. Above it, her son, the Emperor Constantine, erected a succession of splendid buildings, which formed a rectangle thirty yards broad and one hundred and thirty yards long. Across the entire width, a flight of steps led into a pillared courtyard in front of a five-aisled basilica, from the apse of which one descended into the Chapel of

25   The Chapel Above the Holy Sepulchre

56

Coptic Priest

27   *Chapel of the Tombs of Nicodemus and Joseph of Arimathaea*

30 *Crusader Courtyard of the Palace of the Knights Hospitallers*   31 *In the Moslem Quarter*

32   *Ruins of the Jewish Quarter*

the Discovery of the Cross, deep inside the rock. Adjoining the basilica lay another pillared courtyard, which enclosed the site of Golgotha, and from there one entered the huge rotunda built over the Sepulchre of Christ, which lay at its centre.

The Church of the Holy Sepulchre was consecrated in 335 with the participation of all Christendom. Dignitaries of the western churches — which at that time were still united — as well as of the Armenian, Syrian and Coptic churches assembled for the ceremony.

The Church of the Holy Sepulchre was to suffer even more and for a longer period than other shrines. We are already familiar with the inexorable sequence of devastations. It appears that the Persians did not destroy the complex to the same extent as they had done on Mount Zion, since it was possible to restore it to its original form. However, the work of destruction ordered by Caliph Hakim in the 11th century was thorough in the extreme; only the magnificent Rotunda remained untouched. Following this, the individual sites were marked by small chapels. The Crusaders then incorporated them into one dignified edifice which was, of course, much smaller than the original buildings erected by Constantine. It was completed in 1149 on the occasion of the fiftieth anniversary of the Christian Kingdom of Jerusalem. By and large, it conforms with the present layout. In 1808, the rotunda, which till then had remained intact, was burnt almost to the ground — this has been attributed to the carelessness of a tipsy Greek monk — and was rebuilt by the Greeks in its present, unfortunately very clumsy form. The Greek Katholikon is devoid of artistic interest. As if devastation by the hand of man were not sufficient, an earthquake endangered the entire complex in 1927, and the Crusader façade and the interior of the rotunda had to be propped up.

Today one enters the church through the courtyard on the western side, whereas the original building by Constantine was entered from the east. In the entrance hall, a red stone plinth close to the floor indicates the spot where the body of Jesus was anointed and wrapped in its shroud. To the right, eighteen steps lead to the site of Golgotha, which belongs partly to the Franciscans and partly to the Greeks. The lamps hang in thick, golden clusters, and mosaics and icons glisten in the flickering light of the little candles lit by every pilgrim. From here one descends into the rotunda, where a marble edicule has been erected over the tomb of Jesus. At the side of the building opposite the entrance, the Copts have a tiny chapel. Behind the pillars lies a circular gallery onto which other chapels open — the Tomb of Nicodemus, which belongs to the Syrians, the Chapel of Longinus, the Chapel of Mary Magdalen, the chapel on the site where Roman soldiers threw dice for the robe of Jesus, the Chapel of the Mockery of Christ, of the Prison.

A wide flight of steps leads down to the beautiful Chapel of St. Helena — belonging to the Armenians — in which the exalted pilgrim is said to have sat while the Cross was discovered in the shrine lying still deeper down in the rock, originally an old cistern. Roman Catholics, Greek Orthodox, Armenians, Syrians and the Egyptian Copts share the premises, along with the right to hold services, to maintain the chapel and to reside there — rights acquired by virtue of having been present at the consecration over sixteen hundred years ago.

The courtyard of the Church of the Holy Sepulchre is bordered by a Greek monastery and a mosque — the actual Mosque of Omar. During the Caliph's stay in Jerusalem, the Patriarch Sophronius took him through the Church of the Holy Sepulchre.

During the visit, the call of the Muezzin from the outside was heard. Sophronius invited the Caliph to say his prayers in the church, but the Moslem ruler courteously declined, observing that the Moslems might declare the site on which the Caliph had prayed to be a shrine of Islam and requisition it for themselves. He ordered his servant to spread his prayer rug outside the church on the spot where the "real" Mosque of Omar was erected to commemorate the event.

The "Muristan"

From the courtyard of the Church of the Holy Sepulchre we reach the "Muristan," the square on which stands the German Church of the Redeemer. The visitor is not tempted to linger — the church and the nearby rectory are squat, heavy constructions, having no relationship to the surroundings. Let us, nevertheless, stop awhile to trace the amazing history of the Muristan. The Church of the Redeemer, which was consecrated in the autumn of 1898 in the presence of the Imperial couple, is not the first German church to stand on this spot. Charlemagne, whose relations with the Caliph of Bagdad are well known, had a church in honour of Mary and a hospice erected here. A document from the year 1030 mentions yet another church: St. Maria Latina. In its vicinity a merchant from Amalfi had a pilgrims' hospice built in 1070, which he entrusted to a religious order. Shortly thereafter a second religious foundation arose, which was run by nuns. Both houses followed the rule of St. Benedict. After the arrival of the Crusaders, the Prior, Father Gerardus, erected a third house. He obtained dispensation from the Benedictine rule and founded a new order, which he named after the nearby little Church of St. John — the Order of St. John, or of the Hospital. Gerardus soon found that the activities to which the community was dedicated, the providing of shelter and care for the pilgrims, no longer sufficed and that military protection was sorely needed for the young and dangerously exposed Christian Kingdom. In recognition of its vital role, the order was soon endowed with abundant financial means and property.

With the consolidation of the kingdom, pilgrimage set in on an unprecedented scale. It was efficiently and profitably organized by the Venetians. In the course of time the existing buildings became inadequate and the Knights Hospitallers began the construction of an edifice suited to their needs. Supported by 124 columns and 54 pillars, the building united under its roof the "Castellum" of the knights sergeants and clerics, the "Hospitale" or pilgrims' hostel and the "Domus Infirmorum" or hospital. The "Hospitale" alone had room for one thousand guests. Facing the Church of the Holy Sepulchre, the huge building stretched as far as the bazaar of the Street of David. In the walls, traces of early Gothic arches can still be recognized. It was by far the largest Christian building in the capital. It now was hardly necessary to erect any buildings in the city, apart from churches; not a single Moslem or Jew had survived the conquest and tenants for existing buildings were welcome. However, relations between the Patriarchate and the "Castellum," which was directly under the authority of the Pope, were not at all times unruffled. The Hospitallers would sometimes set the bells of St. Maria Latina ringing wildly during the sermons of the Patriarch.

After his entry into Jerusalem, Salah Eddin took up his quarters in the knights' wing of the palace. After the completion of the withdrawal formalities he handed it over to the Moslem religious authorities.

The Knights of St. John continued their activities in the north of the country until the final collapse of the kingdom in 1291. They then moved to Rhodes and eventually to Malta. The order of St. John, whose first home was the Muristan, still exists.

The Church of St. Maria Latina was turned into a hospital in 1219, and the square has since been known by its Arabic name "Muristan," meaning "Hospital."

The collapse of the kingdom was a catastrophe for the country. To prevent the Franks from returning, the Mameluks systematically destroyed the coastal towns. The river mouths became clogged with sand, the fertile plains turned into swamps and the population retreated into the mountains.

In 1517 the Turks conquered the Mameluk Kingdom, and the greatest of their sultans, Suleiman the Magnificent, had Jerusalem rebuilt. The Sultan himself, however, who rode across Hungary and Austria, never saw the city which he had fortified and adorned in princely fashion.

After his death in 1566, the immense empire went into decline. It fell into the hands of weak successors, and the government was taken over by viziers, favourites and court eunuchs. The provincial governors obtained their posts by shrewdly placed gifts. But since they could never be certain that they would not be replaced by some successful rival at court, they were only interested in squeezing as much as possible out of the increasingly impoverished lands while their luck held good. As the country sank into ever deeper poverty and squalor, its population decreased accordingly, and after a while there were neither enough people to fill such buildings as the Palace of the Hospitallers, nor means to maintain the buildings. Moslem law forbade religious property (Wakf) to be put up for sale unless it was wasteland. There was no alternative but to allow the great edifices to fall into ruin.

In 1868, the Crown Prince of Prussia visited Constantinople, and the Sultan made him the gift of a large building site in the heart of the Holy City — the Muristan. The new church was to conform, as far as was possible, to the original Latina, the foundations of which lay beneath the ruins. Before building could commence, however, it was necessary to perform an undertaking of unforeseen proportions — the piled up masses of earth and stones were in places 26 feet high. The foundations, when they were eventually reached, turned out to be far too weak to support a new building, and new ones of the same proportions were laid out on the bedrock 19 feet deeper. A portal of the original church in passable condition was recovered and later incorporated into the northern wall of the new Church of the Redeemer. A double ornamental window, which possibly dates from the Carolingian period, and an elegant stone doorway apparently from the 11th century, were found in the debris. A two-story cloister certainly belonged to the palace of the Order of St. John. These latter finds were skilfully incorporated into the Rectory.

In the shadows of the great Lutheran complex and of a high minaret, there is a friendly little business district. The tidy lanes are wider than in other parts of the Old City, and the small houses are very neatly constructed of pink stone from Bethlehem and topped by tiled roofs. Gates and passages adorned with columns connect the streets. This is Jerusalem's first modern shopping centre, built at the end of the 19th century in a most charming interpretation of the heavy, contemporary European, late Renaissance style. From pieces of columns, stonework ornamentation and other architectural remains from the piles of rubble on the Muristan, a local dignitary erected a bizarre fountain. Water has never splashed in it — at that time it was too rare a commodity to waste, and today the plumbing is no longer usable. In the immediate vicinity of the attractive streets with their demure provincial elegance lie the narrow, raucous, ever-fascinating and crowded bazaars, the Khan e-Zeit (the "Oil Bazaar," once the column-flanked avenue "Cardo Maximus" that is marked on the Madeba map) and the Street of David, which runs from the Jaffa Gate to the Haram e-Sherif.

The Patriarchates

Since the dedication of the Church of the Holy Sepulchre, the churches represented in it have their own patriarchates in the city. Apart from the church buildings, the patriarchal palace and the administrative offices (they all possess extensive real estate), they run schools, youth organizations, homes for the aged, seminaries and libraries. Each patriarchate, whether it consist of a couple of courtyards or occupies a whole small quarter, is a piece of the distant homeland with its language, its customs and the particular aroma of its cuisine.

Near the Muristan and above the Khan e-Zeit lies the Coptic Patriarchate with its two courtyards. The church, whose interior is covered with enormous scenes of the Gospels, can be viewed at any time. But whoever succeeds in the early hours of the morning in slipping through a narrow, bolted door in the Gothic entrance hall will discover two magnificent fifteenth-century Egyptian altars in a wide, vaulted passageway that might once have belonged to a building of the Holy Sepulchre complex. The altars are carved in wood, constructed in the ingenious oriental manner that utilizes not a single nail, and decorated with the finest ivory inlay — very probably these are the only examples of the famed Coptic altars to be found outside Egypt.

From the same little street that leads from the Khan e-Zeit to the Coptic Patriarchate, one steps through a small door into that of the Abyssinians. Opposite the entrance, the courtyard is bordered by the halved length of a Gothic cloister in which hangs a little carillon. The cells of the amiable, religious men who live here in evangelical poverty stand amid pepper and mulberry trees. The Ethiopian national church is an offspring of the Coptic, which organized it in the 8th century, and the Abyssinians have no share in the Church of the Holy Sepulchre. Through the tiny windows of a small dome in the floor, they can see the lights burning far below in the Chapel of St. Helena.

In the vicinity of the Street of the Christians lies the wide gate of the Greek Orthodox Patriarchate. Here one enters a little Greek island city, a maze of mounting flights of steps that lead into courtyards, passages, terraces and small gardens. All the walls and the woodwork are spotlessly whitewashed, with a generous dash of ultramarine mixed into the paint, so that the entire poetic labyrinth lies in an azure haze. The pale, solemn monks and the rosy-cheeked novices seem to have stepped

34   *In the Bazaar*   35   *View of the City Outside the Walls*

38   *The Synagogue of the Hadassah Hospital*

40   *On the Campus of the Hebrew University*

out of the golden background of the icons that gleam within the little churches. The uppermost flight of steps of the blue island leads to a roof terrace immediately in front of the upper stories of the belfry and the cupolas of the Church of the Holy Sepulchre. The Patriarch resides in a lovely and by no means uncomfortable Turkish palace with a throne room and a richly blooming garden. Schools, seminaries, and offices form a quadrangle around a wide courtyard. Surprisingly, the street front is massively decorated in the heavily grandiose style of the late 19th century.

The Latin Patriarchate, which was built in 1847, is a faultlessly correct building which the genius loci seems to have bypassed.

Completely hidden among the little streets and lanes that lead from the Armenian quarter to the bazaars, lies the Patriarchate of the Syrians with the Monastery of St. Mark. According to Syrian tradition, this is the site of the Last Supper and of the house of the evangelist. The language of the liturgy is ancient Syrian, which is closely related to Aramaic, a late form of Hebrew and the language of the people in the time of Jesus. During the religious service, the worshippers stand with hands upraised, an attitude depicted in old Christian paintings.

Nowhere outside Armenia itself can one get to know the Armenian people and their infinitely rich culture better than in Jerusalem. The Monastery and Patriarchate complex on Mount Zion, with its numerous schools and libraries, its publishing house and social establishments, is a whole district in itself — and the most beautifully laid out in the city. The Cathedral of St. James has no equal outside Armenia. Its wealth of glittering ornamentation — paintings, gilded carvings, lamps, ceramics, inlays of tortoise-shell and mother-of-pearl, stone relief work and wrought-iron balustrades —

blends into the majestic lines of the great domed edifice without in any way disturbing its harmony. Confusion may arise only in the mind of the western connoisseur of art, who will find elements of apparently contradictory styles united here in a puzzling and yet enchanting manner. For the Armenians lived along the great roads that led from China, Persia, India and Iraq to Constantinople; they also maintained relations with Rome, Venice and, at a later time, with Amsterdam. With the creative ability peculiar to themselves, they experimented with the elements of every style that passed before their eyes, making use of them to enrich their own tradition. No other people combine the heritage of Byzantium — in the broadest sense — with a distinctly Western mental attitude. The visitor will discover not only that he can converse easily with the Armenians, but that he shares a common language with them in more than a philological sense.

The Ruins of the Jewish Quarter

Until 1948 an extensive Jewish quarter existed within the city walls. For centuries the Jews of the Diaspora sent contributions so that prayers could be recited and the law studied in the holy places. Almost every Jewish community, from Yemen to central Europe and Russia, had its cluster of dwellings and place of worship. It was a little world full of bustling activity and endless learned debates, with domed synagogues and tiny prayer nooks, a world of cabalistic mysteries and esoteric relationships, but also with its ancient and modern social institutions — colourful, mysterious and intimate. The spoken idiom varied from street to street, since Hebrew was used almost solely for the study of Scripture and for prayer.

During the War of Independence in 1948, both army and civilian inhabitants desperately defended the city until the order was given to abandon the Old City after the Jordanians had promised to permit the withdrawal of the civilian population and to treat the defenders according to the Geneva Convention. Although there was absolutely no reason to do so, the quarter was then dynamited. Only the beautiful residential buildings of the Dutch and German communities remained relatively undamaged, so that they could later be restored. The rest of the quarter will be rebuilt in the course of the next few years.

Below this quarter of the city stands the Western Wall, as it came to be called after the time of Solomon. In later time it has been called simply "the Wall" — "Hakotel" in Hebrew. Who would wish to call it the "Wailing Wall" today? Fifteen rows of ashlars still lie beneath the ground. Excavations are under way, and the area in front of it is hot and dusty. Before long, it will be planted with greenery.

The Nineteenth Century

The 19th century began to assert itself in 1846. Until then the city and the people knew only the misery of Turkish exploitation.

The Albanian Muhammed Ali gained control of Egypt in the late 18th century. His son Ibrahim later conquered Palestine. After centuries of senseless misrule, the reins of government passed into the hands of a man whose primary aim was the development of the country. His first step was to abolish immigration restrictions for Christians and Jews and to open the country to Europeans. Christian organizations, in the main, joyfully took advantage of the opportunity to settle in the Holy Land. (In 1839 only five lay Europeans were living in Jerusalem.) The Church of England developed its complex of buildings around Christ Church, opposite the citadel, in 1847. One year later, a Catholic patriarch took up residence in Jerusalem for the first time since 1187. Until then, the Franciscans, as the only Roman Catholic order, more often than not under the most severe conditions and endless vexations, had guarded the sanctuaries and housed the pilgrims.

Even the craft of masonry had been forgotten in the impoverished city. Within the walls land was tilled and vegetables were grown; empty houses served as rubbish dumps. Workers from Malta were brought in to instruct the people, who proved themselves to be extremely apt pupils. In 1854 the first small residential settlements arose outside the city walls, founded by the Jewish philanthropists Sir Moses Montefiore from England and Abraham Touro from New Orleans. Nevertheless it was only with difficulty that people could be induced to live there. Marauders made it dangerous to leave the safety of the city walls, and there was a fear of demons, should one stray beyond the sacred enclosure of the Holy City. The first courageous citizens to move into the neat little dwellings would return to the city in the evening for security.

During the following sixty years, hardly a year went by without at least one important institution being opened inside or outside the city walls. Schools, orphanages, hospitals and other social establishments were attached to the monasteries and mission houses. European countries opened consulates. At the beginning of the 1860's, the Russian Consulate was erected on the former Turkish parade ground, with extensive pilgrim hospices around a large church. Tens of thousands of Russian pilgrims, mostly of poor peasant origin and from all parts of the immense Czarist empire, would arrive in the Holy Land at Christmas, wrapped in furs and spreading a scent of pickled cucumbers and herrings, to remain in Jerusalem until the end of the Easter celebrations. The British consul actively supported the construction of a further Jewish quarter, "Mea She'arim" (Hundred Gates), which to this day is the centre of extreme Jewish orthodoxy.

In 1873 a messianic group from Wurttemberg, the "Templars," who already had several flourishing establishments in the country, settled in the Valley of Rephaim to the southwest of the walls. The large complex of Notre Dame de France was opened opposite the New Gate in 1880. The story of the Swedish group is vividly told in Selma Lagerlöf's book *Jerusalem*. At about the same time, a particularly fine and comfortable "American Colony" was established, also organized along religious lines.

It is not possible to mention every institution here, since there was hardly a single Catholic or Protestant order or religious movement that was not represented in Jerusalem. The purely missionary work of the humanitarian institutions had little success; it was in rebuilding the city that they fulfilled their greatest task. Of particular significance for the further development of both city and country was the orphanage founded by the German Pastor Schneller, the technical schools run by the Franciscan "Terra Santa", and the German colony, since young people were trained by these groups in modern methods of agriculture and the various trades and crafts.

The great Jewish organizations and national communities also participated in the work of reconstruction — chief among them being the "Hilfsverein der Deutschen Juden" and the French "Alliance Israélite."

The handsome, stately new districts outside the city walls grew apace, while the empty spaces in the Old City lanes filled up. Jerusalem was spared the architectural excesses that were proliferating in Europe. The fine natural stone and well-fitted masonry gave the city grace and dignity. Only Kaiser Wilhelm eventually imposed his massive Teutonic excrescences.

This vigorous development, in which local authorities took no part at all, evolved against an absurd political background. The Sublime Porte had progressively become an arena in which the power struggles of the European nations were being waged. It was not pure altruism that lay behind the willingness with which every request for a cash loan was met by these nations. When the time for repayment arrived, the perpetually bankrupt government could see no way out of its dilemma other than by handing over the tax-collecting rights over proportionate territories to the consul of the relevant great power. In addition to this, the consuls of France, Italy and Spain were the official protectors of the Roman Catholic Christians, and Great Britain protected the Jews. Newly arrived immigrants were subject to the consul of their land of origin. All these citizens were excluded from Turkish jurisdiction, and the local landowners availed themselves of every opportunity to achieve a relationship of friendly dependence with a European consulate. Only those who could manage nothing else were directly subordinated to the Pasha and his officials.

This all but incredible manner of government functioned well enough — somewhat similarly to a peaceful federation. At all events, it enabled a rapid recovery of the city, which had been connected with the plain by a fine highway since 1869, and by a railroad since 1892, and which could once again claim its place on the map of the world.

The Mandate

The First World War was a period of dire hardship for Jerusalem. Most of the Europeans were forced to leave the country. Only the Germans, who were the allies of the Turks, were allowed to remain. Palestine became a theatre of war; hunger and epidemics stalked Jerusalem. Though not menaced by the fighting, it was cut off from the fertile plains and the ports. On December 9, 1917, the exhausted city surrendered to the troops of the British General Allenby. The victors were both reverent and eminently humane. Their first concern was to bring up food and medical supplies, and to see that the public services were operating again as efficiently as possible in the circumstances. The commandant, Sir Ronald Storrs, was deeply conscious of the particular significance of his post. Bedevilled by seemingly numberless problems, whose solution was further complicated by the multiplicity of ethnic groups and their conflicting claims and peculiarities, he never forgot what was dear to his heart: the preservation of the beauty and dignity of the city he loved so deeply. He created a building commission which took care that neither cement nor corrugated iron should be used in The Old City and supervised the reconstruction and restoration of the historical monuments as soon as this was expedient. His hope that the ceramic facings of the Dome of the Rock be renovated by Armenian artists was not fulfilled, since the necessary funds could not be raised. Nevertheless, the master potters whom he brought in from Turkey introduced an art form which enriched the city with a particularly charming and still flourishing craft.

In 1920, the military administration was replaced by the British Mandate. In 1917, before the decisive outcome of World War I, Palestine was promised to the Jews by Britain as a national home — with the proviso that the rights of the non-Jewish communities would be respected. The "Balfour Declaration" was received by Jews all over the world with deep gratitude. The Zionist colonists had already created a network of rural settlements and urban communities, and when Britain appointed Sir Herbert Samuel, a former cabinet minister and a practicing Jew, as High Commissioner of the mandated territory, the generous gesture acquired added significance. Lord Samuel took up residence in the Auguste Victoria Hospice, since the government house to the south of the city had not yet been built.

The non-Jewish population, however, did not share in the jubilation. The noble but ambiguous formulation of the "Balfour Declaration" led to the disturbances which broke out during the very next year and which were to characterize to an ever greater extent the period of the Mandate. Despite these troubles, a steady stream of Jewish immigrants began to arrive, mainly from Russia and Poland at first. After the difficult early-postwar years, it was once again possible to raise extensive funds for the work of reconstruction in Palestine, and this work was by no means limited to the Jewish sectors alone. The consuls reoccupied their posts, the clergy their monasteries and a devoted civil service the old houses and handsome new villas. In 1925 the Hebrew

University was inaugurated on Mount Scopus. The King David Hotel was already standing to accommodate guests of honour, and a little later the striking building of the Y.M.C.A. arose, to be followed by the Zionist Organization building on the edge of the new residential district of Rehavia. Garden suburbs sprang up around the city. Greeks, Armenians, Syrians and Abyssinians built rows of houses on their properties. Scientific institutes (in particular for archaeology), colleges, libraries and museums were opened. The public services functioned well, and in 1936 the broadcasting station was completed. Immigration from Germany, which brought numerous university graduates into the country, promoted a new standard of urban culture. Theatre and cabaret ensembles from Tel-Aviv came to perform in Jerusalem, as did the orchestra, honoured by such distinguished guest conductors as Toscanini and such virtuosos as Hubermann, Jascha Heifetz and Harriet Cohen. A ballet group was formed which was much patronized, and all these events were discussed in the new continental cafés over Viennese coffee and excellent pastry. The Old City with its captivating charm and the carefully laid-out and expanding new city could have complemented each other so well; nowhere could life have been more fascinating, more inspiring and more colourful, had the sound of gunfire and exploding grenades not become so frequent, the inflammatory propaganda so vicious, and the mutual respect and tolerance of the various ethnic groups so deeply undermined. The government, which had acted against the terrorists more symbolically than effectively, gained control of the situation only at the outbreak of the Second World War, when the violence and unrest could no longer be tolerated.

Jerusalem became a centre for the Allies and a leave station for the troops in the

Mediterranean theatre of war. Thus this dreadful period was a time of economic renewal for Palestine. However, the prosperous situation could not be enjoyed to the full, since the British and the Jews were both weighed down by the terrible events affecting their peoples in Europe.

With the conclusion of the war, the troubles began again and became more widespread. Increased restrictions on Jewish immigration were the result of Arab pressure on the British, and were now directed against the desperate survivors of the extermination camps in Europe. Jewish bitterness vented itself in acts of terrorism against the British. Part of the King David Hotel, the Zionist Organization building and even whole stretches of streets were destroyed by bombs. Despite strong military reinforcements, the government could only react with reprisals, executions and harassment. Barbed-wire fences divided the Jewish areas, and insane emergency laws were passed. Invisible barriers, however, had long separated Jewish and Arab districts. Ditties that the children on both sides of the barriers chanted while skipping rope or playing hop-scotch were macabre parodies of the customary nursery rhymes. On May 14, 1948 the Union Jack was lowered for the last time from its mast on the High Commissioner's palace. Jerusalem had, in fact, long been a divided city.

The services performed by the mandatory government should by no means be underrated. The political challenge would have been beyond any government. Much of lasting value was achieved in administration, building, communications and health services. In the field of urban planning the thirty-year period of the Mandate was particularly beneficial. Monuments were carefully restored and maintained, and elegant and harmonious new buildings arose along well-laid-out streets.

90

In November 1947, the General Assembly of the United Nations decided on the division of Palestine into an Arab and a Jewish state. A special status was to be created for Jerusalem. The Mandate, if not renewed, was to end on May 15, 1948. The Jewish people supported the U. N. decision with enthusiasm, but the Arabs rejected it unconditionally. Unrest now flared into guerilla warfare. On May 14, the State of Israel was proclaimed in Tel-Aviv, since the capital was cut off from the rest of the country and under heavy fire. The front ran through the city from south to north.

The Capital of Israel

When the first cease-fire was arranged after six weeks of fighting, no international forum could have altered the situation in any way. The Old City and the northern district were taken over by Jordan. In addition to the western districts of the city, which were almost entirely built and inhabited by Jews, the Israeli army had occupied the southern suburbs. The front became the frontier.

Jerusalem now lay on the tip of a salient that jutted deep into Jordan, so that it was surrounded on three sides and connected with the rest of the country only by the mountainous "Jerusalem Corridor." Despite this unfavourable position it would have been unthinkable to proclaim another city as capital.

It was a considerable time before the city recovered from the murderous six-week siege and the streets became animated and gardens blossomed again. Only gradually did the government occupy its offices. Light industry had to be created to ensure an economic basis for the admission of new immigrants, and the city was thus finally drawn into the vigorous development process of the young state. New residential blocks were erected, then merged into quarters and linked up with old suburbs. Rural settlements were built in the "Corridor." The university carried on in empty convent schools and mission houses until the first new faculty buildings in the west stood ready in 1954. Then followed the new building of the Hadassah Hospital outside the city. In 1965 the Israel Museum was opened, and in the following year parliament at last moved into a building worthy of receiving it. Since 1958 a wonderful park has been brightening the centre of the city — a gift from South Africa's Jews (just one example of the way in which Jewry as a whole participated in the work of reconstruction and also provided the means to erect representative public buildings).

The surroundings of the city began to turn green as the newly-planted Jerusalem Forest began to cover the rocky slopes. A generation grew up thinking it not at all unusual that the world should end in the centre of the city before a cement wall or a barbed-wire entanglement and that an entire city belt with its fine houses should fall into ruin behind these barricades—no man's land; while in other areas only a wire fence separated the countries, the border sentries on either side could stare into each other's eyes and the Israeli and Jordanian housewives could almost sniff each other's cooking pots. They were accustomed to the firing of shots and the wounding and killing of people. For a couple of steps too far, eastwards, could mean the end of a human life. Their parents told them how they had walked through the colourful bazaars to the Temple Wall. From the southern suburbs one could see the cupola of the

Dome of the Rock, and from the roofs in the west could watch the bustling activity at Damascus Gate.

And those who could still visit there! With frank envy — and the older ones with nostalgia — the Israelis saw clergy, tourists, diplomats and officials of the United Nations pass through the Mandelbaum Gate, which was closed to them. A successful haberdasher of this name, who had acquired property there, went down very unwillingly into history.

As could easily be seen with the naked eye, building activity "over there" was likewise intense. The great hotels and new suburbs towards the north looked exactly the same as "over here." "A stupid situation. How long can this last?" was frequently heard, with a sigh. But there was little reason to hope.

Never less so than at the outbreak of the 1967 war. When the first pieces of shrapnel from the east scattered over the city, the children were at school, the students — at least those who had not yet been called up — were at their lectures, the government offices and the shops were open, and a last appeal had been sent to King Hussein through the United Nations. It went unheeded. For two days and a night, the civilian population of both parts of Jerusalem sat in the shelters, while the Israeli army tightened its encirclement of the city through Samaria in the south and Hebron in the north, finally fighting its way through the Mandelbaum Gate and the Valley of Kidron to reach the Old City. "The Wall" . . . "the Wall" . . . it suddenly seemed as if the entire campaign concerned only the Wall — as if one had waited nineteen, no, one thousand eight hundred and ninety-seven years for this moment. The Wall . . . some broke into cheers and embraced one another, some stood as if in a daze, unable to comprehend. Some who remembered it from their childhood, and the youngest ones who had never seen it — and who often enough had declared that stones were only stones and that was that — laid their faces against these stones as against their mother's knees, stroking them as the cheeks of their beloved one. Following an ancient custom, worshippers inserted small pieces of paper, with their deepest wishes written on them, between the stones of the wall. (General Moshe Dayan was the first to place a little folded page between the blocks. It is said there was only a single word written on it: "Shalom"—peace.) Then they recited the prayers of thanksgiving — "... that He allowed us to know this hour, to reach it and to celebrate it," and the great praise of God, life and peace, the Kaddish, the Jewish prayer for the dead. They prayed it for those who had not reached the wall, whose blood stained the paving stones of the narrow streets and who heard no more the ram's horn wailing and the jubilation from the Temple Wall.

Eight days later the Feast of Pentecost (Shavuoth) was celebrated. After nineteen years the first pilgrimage to the Western Wall took place. It was still a carefully marked path that led partly through minefields — a long, hot road. But who would have complained? It was a day out of a psalm. "We were as dreamers..." Two hundred thousand people flocked to the wall on that day.

In the following weeks the barricades and the ruins of no man's land were razed. These included dilapidated rows of buildings that partly concealed the city wall, which now stands free and proud as in the days of Sultan Suleiman.

The final reunification, however, took place on June 29 at midday, when the gates of the city were opened for free traffic in both directions. Naturally enough, everybody was burning with eagerness to see what it looked like "over there." It almost seemed as if the city had been divided again: the Arabs streamed through the western quarters, and the Jews through the Old City and the eastern new city. It often happened that while the crowds mingled, people no longer young stopped, looked at each other questioningly and then embraced with beaming faces. "You managed to get through it all right? Did you have a good shelter, water, supplies? Did your home remain safe? What do you think will happen now? Will it be peace, salaam, shalom at last? We waited so long . . ." They were the same questions in Hebrew as in Arabic.

Yet the two parts of Jerusalem could not be joined together as easily as the two halves of a broken bowl. It was indeed not to be expected that old loyalties could be discarded from one day to the next. There seemed to be no end to the problems; those of a technical nature, though complicated enough, were by far the easiest to solve. There was a school problem, the different types of administration and legislation, the language question, the monetary system, to name only the most pressing ones.

At first administration was halting and haphazard. Then it began to work more smoothly and efficiently as people began to get acquainted and to trust each other. The civil service was gradually integrated and the municipal offices divided up over the now united city. One after the other the Arab schools opened for the new scholastic year. With equal zeal the citizens of Jerusalem enrolled in the Arabic and Hebrew courses held by the authorities.

Archaeologists whose names were well known throughout the world came to the traditional autumn congress which this year naturally took place in Jerusalem and had Jerusalem as its theme. Thirty Arab students entered the Hebrew University. The municipal youth orchestra was increased by an Arab group, which performs with Jewish boys and girls on official occasions as well as playing Arab music. These are only a few examples from the everyday life of a great human experiment, the success of which could be of world-wide significance. Is it mere coincidence that this is being undertaken in Jerusalem?

"Wish Jerusalem Peace!" (Psalm 122).

1 *The Citadel,* on the western side of the city wall above the Valley of Hinnom, was rebuilt in 1335. The minaret of the garrison mosque, popularly known as the "Tower of David," is of 16th century origin.

2 *The Church of the Dormition on Mount Zion,* which belongs to the Benedictines, stands on the traditional site of the "Falling Asleep of Mary" and of the descent of the Holy Ghost. In the year 390 the magnificent basilica of Hagia Zion was built here, which became known as the "Mother of All Churches." From the left-hand tower projection of the present-day church, the basilica once extended over the site of the small building on the right with the minaret, which houses the Hall of the Last Supper, above the so-called "Tomb of David." The building was transformed by the Turks into a Moslem shrine, "Nebi Da'oud" (the Prophet David), in the 16th century. The modern Church of the Dormition was consecrated in 1910. The terrain, a gift to Kaiser Wilhelm from the Sultan, was presented to the Archbishop of Cologne. To the left, the city wall

can be seen, and in the foreground, above the Valley of Hinnom, the houses of the district of Yemin Moshe, the oldest settlement outside the walls, which was erected by the Jewish philanthropist Sir Moses Montefiore. In the background the Hotel Intercontinental stands on the southern peak of the Mount of Olives.

3 *The Hall of the Last Supper (Coenaculum).* The only Roman Catholic order to remain in the Holy Land after the fall of the Kingdom of Jerusalem in 1291 was the Order of St. Francis, which held on in spite of appalling conditions and constant persecution. In 1335 the Franciscan Friars were able to build a small monastery on Mount Zion, and in 1347 they erected this hall beside it, over the traditional site of the Last Supper and the ruins of the earlier chapel. The artisans are believed to have come from Cyprus. The prayer niche blocking the centre window was installed in 1926. Although no longer in use as such, the Coenaculum is still *de jure* a mosque, and no Christian religious services may be held there.

4 *The Southeast Section of the Wall,* with a view into the city showing the wall of Haram e-Sherif, the one-time Temple district, with the Aksa Mosque. In the background is the Mount of Olives. The city wall and the gates were erected by order of Suleiman the Magnificent towards the middle of the 16th century, mainly on the foundations of the Herodian city wall.

5 *View of the Southeast Corner of the Wall from the Valley of Kidron.* The massive ashlars of the Herodian period are clearly distinguishable from the later masonry.

6 *On the Mount of Olives.* In the foreground stands the "Church of the Agony," which was consecrated in 1924, the Garden of Gethsemane and the Russian Church of Mary Magdalene, built by Czar Alexander III and consecrated in 1885.

7 *In the Garden of Gethsemane.* The grove of ancient olive trees belongs to the Franciscans and is open to all visitors.

8 *A Greek Orthodox Novice in the Tomb of Mary.* Deep inside the mountain lies the Tomb of Mary, which was chiselled out of the rock. Although originally looked after by the Franciscans, the Friars were forced to hand it over to the Greek Orthodox Church in the 18th century. Both Greek and Oriental orthodox religious services are celebrated here, but out of protest no Catholic service is held. The Moslems, who revere the Mother of Jesus as "Sittna Mariam" (Our Lady Mary), also have a place of prayer here.

9 *The Temple Mount* above the Valley of Kidron, seen from the Mount of Olives at sunrise. In the centre of the "Haram e-Sherif" – the Exalted Enclave – rises the Dome of the Rock – "Kubbet e-Ssakhra, after the sanctuaries in Mecca and Medina the holiest shrine of Islam. To the left is the Aksa Mosque, standing against the southern stretch of wall. The hill on the far left of the picture on which the small houses stand is the site of the Jebusite city which was conquered by David. Above it is seen the Church of the Dormition on Mount Zion.

10   *Jewish Mausoleums from the Hasmonean Period*, on the southern slope of the Mount of Olives. They date from the 2nd and 1st centuries B.C.

11   *The Lions' Gate* above the Valley of Kidron is the only entrance to the city from the east. Behind it begins the Via Dolorosa. The shell scars date from the "Six-Day War" of June 1967.

12   *"Haram e-Sherif,"* the former Temple Area. Below and to the right stands the Western Wall of the Herodian Temple Area (the Wailing Wall). In the background is the Valley of Kidron and the Mount of Olives.

13   *The Dome of the Rock* encloses the rock from which the Prophet Muhammed rose up to stand before the face of God. It was built in 695 by the Ommyad Caliph Abd el-Malik. The ceramic ornamentation, which was restored several times, was originally presented by Sultan Suleiman the Magnificent. The name "Mosque of Omar" is doubly a misnomer; the

Dome of the Rock is neither a mosque – the religious services are held in the Aksa Mosque – nor is it connected with anyone by the name of Omar. The similarity of the charming little "Dome of the Chain" on the left, which was built at the same time as the Dome of the Rock, is misleading, for not eight, but eleven columns support the outer roof, and six support the cupola. They are so arranged that all seventeen columns are visible at a single glance. In the foreground stands one of the numerous little edifices – minor shrines, prayer niches, pulpits and fountains – that are scattered all over the Temple Area.

14   *The Solemn Friday Service in the Aksa Mosque.* The numerous alterations and restorations which the Mosque has undergone in the course of its history are immediately apparent in the lack of uniformity in the architecture. The central part still clearly shows traces of the 6th century triple-aisled basilica, on the ruins of which the Mosque was erected in the following century. (The church in honour of Mary built by Justinian was destroyed in 614 by the Persians.) At that time two side aisles were added to obliterate the cruciform shape of the ground plan. During the period

99

of the Christian Kingdom of Jerusalem, the Mosque is said to have served as the royal palace from the conquest in 1099. In 1118 it was handed over to the newly founded order of the Knights Templars as headquarters and mother church of the order. After the conquest of the city by Salah Eddin in 1187, the Sultan added the mosaic ornamentation. The columns are of recent date, and the ceiling is a gift from the late King Farouk.

15 *The Damascus Gate,* the most ornate of the eight city gates, situated on the north side of the city wall, leads to the bazaars.

16 *The Church of St. Anne,* built towards the middle of the 12th century, is one of the most lovely buildings from the period of the Crusades. Tradition has it that the church stands over the house of Mary's birth. Nearby is the site of the pool of Bethesda, where Jesus healed the paralytic. The property is owned by the White Fathers. Since the church lies directly behind the Lions' Gate, one of the main targets of the recent fighting, it was damaged by shell-fire; repairs are currently being effected.

17 *View of the Old City Towards the East.* To the left is the dome over the rotunda of the Church of the Holy Sepulchre and the smaller one of the Greek "Katholikon," beside it the bell-tower built by the Crusaders. The rotunda stands on the foundations of the complex that was built by the Emperor Constantine and consecrated in 335, and that extended towards the east. The flight of steps to the entrance lay approximately beneath the large building in the centre of the picture (above the minaret and the long roof). The atrium was adjoined by a basilica that led into a pillared courtyard in which was the site of Golgotha (beneath the roof to the right between the two cupolas). Here one entered the rotunda above the Holy Sepulchre. The circular building occupied the width of the complex. To the right is the Lutheran Church of the Redeemer, which follows the outline of the earlier Church of St. Maria Latina, built on the same spot in 1070. It was consecrated in 1898 in the presence of the German Imperial couple. Beside it stand the rectory and the new school of the Lutheran World Association. Rectory, school and the buildings in front of them with the tiled roofs stand on the square that was once occupied by the enormous palace of

the Order of St. John, which was opened in 1140 and which extended about 110 yards further to the right. Between the Holy Sepulchre and the Church of the Redeemer is the "real" Mosque of Omar with its minaret – to the right above the northern part of the Haram e-Sherif. Below it runs the Via Dolorosa, which curves around the long building on the far left, then leads past the row of houses towards the left edge of the picture, again curves to the right and finally leads through the courtyard between the minaret and the bell-tower into the Church of the Holy Sepulchre. In the background on the left-hand side is the Rockefeller Museum, above it Mount Scopus, on which (in the centre) the "Auguste Victoria" building stands, and to the right the Mount of Olives.

18 *The "Prison of Christ,"* above which a Greek Orthodox monastery stands, lies near the Ecce Homo Arch on the Via Dolorosa. The corridors and chambers are carefully hewn out of the solid rock and once belonged to the subterranean part of the Herodian fortress of Antonia, which bordered on the present-day Via Dolorosa.

19 *The Via Dolorosa with the "Ecce Homo Arch."* The first station on the path to Calvary is the "Flagellation," the Church of the Scourging. The "Ecce Homo Arch" belongs to the central part of a tripartite gateway erected by the Emperor Hadrian in the 2nd century B.C. The left-hand side of the arch is now within the church of the convent of the Sisters of Zion.

20 *On the Via Dolorosa.* Numerous handicraft, souvenir and antique shops, and shops selling religious articles line the Via Dolorosa. The richly embroidered Judean peasant dresses – such as are worn by the Fellaha woman in the picture – are eagerly bought by visitors.

21 *Candle Stall Outside the Courtyard of the Church of the Holy Sepulchre.* The tiny, colourful stalls at which pilgrims can purchase candles, incense and religious souvenirs become more and more numerous the closer one comes to the Holy Sepulchre. The many-coloured spade-shaped candles with the golden ornamentation are a local specialty.

22 *The Crusader Façade of the Church of the Holy Sepulchre.* The present-day form of the Church of the Holy Sepulchre is essentially based on the reconstruction by the Crusaders, which was completed for the fiftieth anniversary celebrations of the Christian Kingdom of Jerusalem in 1149. Now as then, the Roman Catholic, Greek Orthodox, Syrian, Armenian and Coptic Churches share in its possession and hold religious services there.

23 *The Chapel of St. Helena.* Armenian religious service.

24 *The Golgotha Altar in the Church of the Holy Sepulchre* belongs to the Greek Orthodox Church.

25 *Chapel Above the Holy Sepulchre* in the centre of the rotunda. The rotunda in its present form and the chapel over the Holy Sepulchre were built by the Greeks after a fire had destroyed the original edifice in 1808. Greek Orthodox, Armenian Orthodox and Roman Catholic masses are celebrated daily at appointed times. The Roman Catholic Church is represented by the Franciscans.

26 *Coptic Priest* in the tiny Coptic chapel in the rear wall of the Holy Sepulchre.

27 *Chapel of the Tombs of Nicodemus and Joseph of Arimathaea* in the possession of the Syrian Orthodox Church. Sitting at the wall is the Patriarch.

28 *The Church of the Abyssinian Monastery* above the court of the Church of the Holy Sepulchre.

29 *The Armenian Cathedral of St. James* is the main church.

30 *Crusader Courtyard of the Palace of the Knights Hospitallers of the order of St. John,* built into the Lutheran Rectory.

31 *In the Moslem Quarter.* An antique archway serves as a frame for an old Arab fountain.

32 *Ruins of the Jewish Quarter.* After the evacuation of the Jewish inhabitants during the war of 1948, the Jordanians destroyed the Jewish quarter of the Old City with its schools, social institutions and places of worship. Reconstruction of this area is now being planned.

33 *Religious Service at the Western Wall.* The stones employed by Hadrian to restore the wall can be clearly distinguished from the massive original blocks of the Herodian period.

34 *In the Bazaar.* One of the most successful inventions of the Orient are the sheltered shopping centres, the bazaars. With all the crowding, hustle and bustle and occasional quarrels, they are nevertheless full of charming, dusky intimacy. There are no quick bargains here: the shopkeeper appreciates a discriminating customer and is always ready for a chat; fun is a part of business, as is the conclusion of a transaction that follows age-old rules. Even the purchase of a couple of pounds of vegetables requires a poetic exchange of compliments and courteous formulas. The Khan e-Zeit (the Oil Bazaar) runs southward from the Damascus Gate, following the course of the former "Cardo Maximus," the road lined with columns, which appears on the 6th century Madeba Mosaic Map.

35 *View of the City Outside the Walls.* To the right of the large building above the supermarket is seen the Y.M.C.A. with its tower; behind it stands the King David Hotel. On the far side of the Valley of Kidron and above it rises Mount Zion with the Church of the Dormition. To the left of this lies the city wall, behind which are the gardens and cupolas of the Armenian quarter and then the Citadel. Following is the cupola of the Dome of the Rock and the steeple of the Lutheran Church of the Redeemer; then comes the rooftop of the Latin Patriarchate directly behind the city wall, followed by the tower of the Franciscan Church of San Salvatore on the border of the northern section of the wall. Below and to the left is the entrance to the city park. In the background is Mount Scopus with the "Auguste Victoria" building erected by Kaiser Wilhelm II, and the Mount of Olives.

36 *United Jerusalem.* Arab and Jewish citizens and peasant women from the surrounding villages wait for a 'bus.

37 *Market in the Mea She'arim Quarter,* the strictly conservative Jewish Section.

38 *The Synagogue of the Hadassah Hospital* with the stained-glass windows by Marc Chagall. Each of the twelve windows contains symbols and historical motifs of one of the twelve tribes of Israel. (Here Naftali, Joseph and Benjamin.)

39 *The Ancient Monastery of the Cross and the Israel Museum.* The Monastery of the Cross lay far from the city in the solitude of the mountains when it was founded by Georgian monks at the end of the 5th century. According to legend it was in this valley that the tree grew from which the wood for the cross of Christ was cut. Today the western suburbs of the city extend up to the "Valley of the Cross." Opposite lies the Israel Museum, which was opened in 1965 and has departments of pre-history, archaeology, Jewish religious and folk art, modern painting and graphic art, and a sculpture garden. In the background is the campus of the university.

40 *The Hebrew University* was founded on Mount Scopus in 1925. After the war of 1948, it was no longer accessible, and lecture halls, laboratories, and libraries had to be improvised in empty buildings of which there were sufficient in Jerusalem at that time, so that no academic year was lost. In 1954, the first faculty buildings were opened on the new campus of "Givat Ram"; since then many new buildings have been added, including the National Library, an amphitheatre, large botanical gardens, student hostels and a synagogue. The old campus on Mount Scopus will also be reoccupied after the buildings have been completely restored, since the number of students is increasing steadily, although branches of the Hebrew University have been opened in the south (Beersheba) and in the north (Haifa) and two universities have been built in Tel-Aviv. The bronze statue is the work of the sculptor Henry Moore.

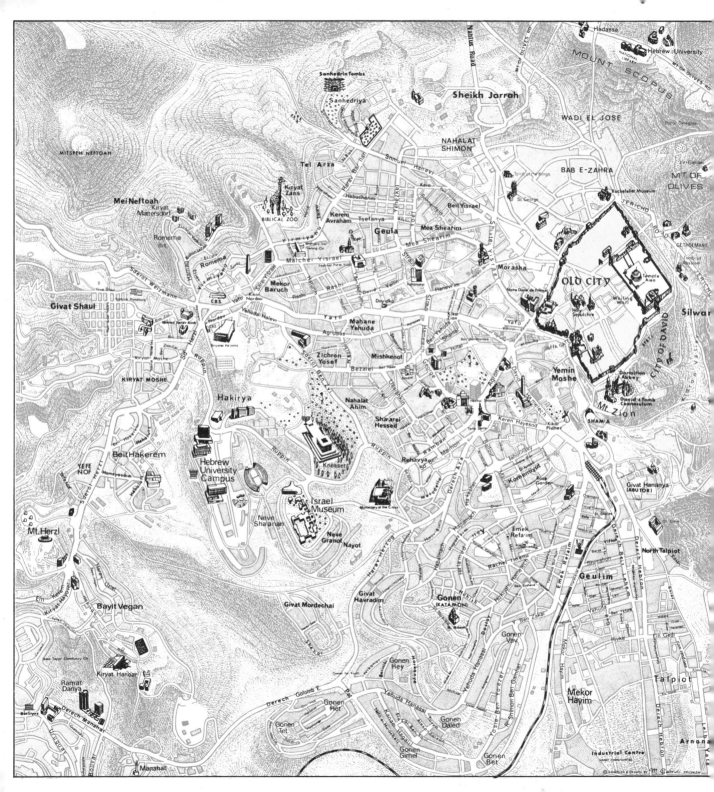